OH NO!
AF421981

Title:Oh No!
Author: Alexis Toran
Illustrator: Alexis Toran

For permission requests, write to the publisher at 1949 Stillwood Lane, Virginia Beach, VA 23456
ISBN: 979-8-3305-3348-0
First Edition: October, 2024
Printed in United States Of America

This Book Belongs To

For my beloved Jahsiah,
your boundless energy and endless curiosity brings
light to every day.
This story is a celebration of the joy, wonder, and
beautiful chaos you bring into my life.
Thank you for being you.

"Wake up, little rascal, it's a brand-new day!"
But he wiggles and squirms and then zooms away.
Mommy sighs and she grins, though she knows what's in store,
"Oh no, not again!" she says with a roar.

"Let's brush those pearly whites!" Mommy says with cheer,
But he hides the toothbrush, a grin ear to ear.
"No brushing for me!" he laughs, running away,
"Oh no!" Mommy sighs, "It's the start of the day!"

Then breakfast time comes, a big milk cup in sight,
But he pushes it back with all his might.
"I won't drink it!" he cries, with a frown and a glare,
"Oh no, not again!" sighs Mom, fixing her stare.

Mommy says, "No! Leave the paper alone!"
But soon the whole house is a toilet paper zone.
He spins and spins like a merry-go-round,
White streams of paper all over the ground!

No veggies for me!" the toddler declares,
Green peas fly high, zooming through the air!
Spinach is squished, carrots get tossed,
But the toddler's happy — The veggies have lost!

His toys scatter wide, all over the floor,
But cleaning them up? That's a "chore-what-for?"
"Not cleaning today!" he shouts with glee,
"Oh no!" Mommy sighs, "Why won't you agree?"

He toddles to the toilet with a mischievous grin,
Mommy shouts, "No, don't throw things in!"
Plop goes a toy, then another and more—
Now rubber ducks float, and blocks line the floor!

Crayons in hand, he draws on the wall,
Red, blue, and green, he's having a ball.
"Oh no!" Mommy gasps, eyes wide in distress,
But he beams with pride, showing Off His Progress

Mommy says, "No, no, no, don't touch that vase!"
But the toddler's giggling, making a face.
He grabs a toy, zooms all around,
Mommy's precious vase hits the ground!

With keys in his hand, he dashes with glee,
And hides them in places only he can see!
"Oh no!" Mommy cries, "Where did my keys go?"
He just giggles, feeling clever because mommy doesn't know!

Off to the car, but he won't take his seat,
Wriggling and kicking, moving his feet. "Oh no!"
Mommy pleads, "sit down, pretty please?" But he's
off on a mission, attempting to flee!

n the grocery store, he makes a big scene,
Throws a tantrum so loud, red, pink, and green!
"Oh no!" Mommy blushes, her cheeks quite red,
As he finally calms down, "Can we go home instead?"

Mommy is tired, hands on her hips,
She says with a smile, "You're full of tricks!"
"No more mess, it's time to rest."
But the toddler's still full of zest!

Mommy, snuggles, please?" he says with a grin,
With eyes so sweet, she can't help but give in.
Mommy sighs, "Alright, come close, my dear,"
Her little one needs cuddles and love, that much is clear

Oh yes," whispers Mommy, her sigh full of love, As her
rascal rests peacefully, snug as a glove.
Mischief's done, but Mommy's love is here to stay,
Tomorrow's another silly day!